BERNARD HÄRING

Our Father

Translation by
Gwen Griffith-Dickson

SAINT MARY'S PRESS
Christian Brothers Publication
Winona, Minnesota

First published in Great Britain in 1996
by MCCRIMMON PUBLISHING CO LTD

This British-American edition of *Our Father* published
in 1996 by SAINT MARY'S PRESS
Christian Brothers Publications,
Winona, Minnesota 55987-1320

ISBN 0-88489-483-5

Cover design by Nick Snode
Typeset in Berling and Fenice by McCrimmons

Reprographics by Anagram Litho Ltd., Southend-on-Sea, Essex
Printed by BPC Wheatons Ltd., Exeter

Contents

'Be perfect as your heavenly
Father is perfect.'

MATTHEW 5:48

Foreword

SINCE the time of the Church Fathers, countless books have sought to expound the *Lord's Prayer*, the inexhaustible bequest of Jesus to his disciples. For the whole of our life to our death, each of us should be, and continue to become, a commentary on the *Lord's Prayer*. We are always growing and seeking our identity in this prayer, which is given to all of us yet assigned uniquely to each of us, at once a prayer of intercession, praise, and a programme for our lives.

A part of my life, my prayer and indeed my own life's programme is interpreted on these pages, if very imperfectly. The reader cannot read and contemplate it without understanding and interpreting it in the light of their own prayer, praise and life's programme. May our voices and hearts resonate in harmony.

I am keeping to the text of the *Lord's Prayer* as it is prayed today in our churches. It is essentially the text of Matthew's Gospel in the middle of the Sermon on the Mount. It stands in the light and the forcefield of the *Beatitudes* and the Counsels of Perfection. It can only develop its liberating and enchanting beauty for us if we, like the disciples at the Sermon on the Mount, gather around Jesus and marvel, grateful, adoring the one who sets out the sevenfold 'Blessed are they'.

Nevertheless we only feel inwardly free and at home in the *Lord's Prayer* when we have already said 'Yes' decisively to the supreme goal, expressed in the lapidary sentence: 'be perfect as your heavenly Father is perfect' *(Matthew 5:48)*. It is revealed in Jesus above all in his non-violent love of his enemies. In the *Our Father* Jesus takes us by the hand, to initiate us in the power of his Holy Spirit into the dignity and truth of our calling as sons and daughters of God: 'love your enemies and pray for them, even those who persecute you, so that you become sons and daughters of your Father in heaven' *(Matthew 5:44)*.

Bernard Häring
Gars-am-Inn, Germany

1: The overview

We hear the voice of the Father

PRAYER is the breath of life of our faith in God, our Father, the Father of our Lord Jesus Christ. But faith comes from hearing. What is the message that comes to us from the Father and enables us and invites us to pray?

As Jesus after his baptism in Jordan 'rose out of the water, he saw the heavens opening and the spirit coming down upon him like a dove. And a voice spoke from heaven: "you are my beloved Son, in whom I am well pleased" *(Matthew 1:9-11)*. These words are the password, the inscription on the four Servant Songs of Deutero-Isaiah *(Isaiah 42:1)*.

At his baptism, Jesus said an irrevocable 'Yes' to his call as a non-violent, suffering Servant of God. He said 'Yes' to a limitless solidarity of salvation with the whole of humanity, but above all with those who would be baptised in his name, who would also commit themselves to his life's programme.

Cyril of Jerusalem said in his catechism on baptism: 'at Jesus' baptism in the Jordan, the voice of the Father resounded: "You are my beloved Son ..." At our baptism the good news is addressed to us: now you have become sons and daughters of God.'

That presupposes, naturally, that we commit ourselves to the programme of all-encompassing love, including loving our enemies, that was chosen by the beloved Son, the faithful Servant of God.

Based on this self-commitment under the guidance of the Spirit of God, this same Spirit takes us into the dignity, the programme and the Abba-prayer of the beloved Son.

Before the *Our Father*, then, comes the sublime message that has never been heard before: that all who commit themselves with Jesus to the cause of messianic peace, to healing, liberating love, are adopted by the Father, the Almighty and All-merciful.

All our prayer, including our whole life's programme, is therefore transported by the wonder, the thanks, the rejoicing over being addressed as sons and daughters by the All-holy God, the creator of heaven and earth, in the sight of Jesus. Our wonder and rejoicing over such a sublime call is essential, but it is clear that this wonder and rejoicing itself is indissolubly bound up with our assent. Our acquiescence takes us up in Jesus' loving and being loved, the assent to precisely that unprecedented, liberating call of Jesus who was prepared to suffer, an assent flows from his love for the Father and for all humanity.

We gather closely around Jesus

In the Sermon on the Mount we see Jesus lead his disciples up to a climax in the *Beatitudes*, a peak bathed in the pure healing light of faith in God as our Father, the Father of our Lord Jesus Christ. 'He sat down and gathered his disciples around him' *(Matthew 5:1)*. Without Jesus we can do nothing towards our salvation and the salvation of the world. Only gathered closely around him, gazing on him in love and trust, with eyes and ears only for him, what he is and what he says, are we initiated into the mystery of Christian prayer.

As Jesus expressly teaches us in the great Abba-prayer *(John 17)*, it is all about knowing Jesus and knowing the Father. 'This is eternal life: to know you, the only true God, and Jesus Christ, the one you have sent' *(John 17:3)*. It is not a question of purely conceptual knowledge, but rather the knowledge of love, of receptive love and the assent to the call to the Kingdom of this love.

Before his surrender to suffering, Jesus rejoiced before his Abba: 'I have made your name known to those whom you took from the world and gave to me. They are yours and you have given them to me' *(John 17:6)*.

Our rejoicing in Abba, gathered closely around Jesus, is not primarily based on our life's programme. First and foremost is what Jesus intended and made over to us: the loving knowledge of the Father through the loving, grateful knowledge of the one the Father sent to us: Jesus Christ.

From this listening, this wonder and thanks then flows an authentic 'Yes' to the programme: our sublime calling as sons and daughters of God, united to Jesus, the saviour of the world.

Rejoicing in the Holy Spirit, wonder, self-giving and thanks are the way in. That belongs to the real heart of the Christian life's programme. Its foundation is not a stern 'Should!' and 'Must!' That creates stress and is condemned to fail if it is placed in the foreground or indeed, does so any time when being overcome with wonder and thanks and rejoicing in the Holy Spirit is not firmly in the foreground.

The *Lord's Prayer*, the *Our Father*, and the prayer of the redeemed generally, does not begin directly with our contribution to the plan of salvation, the will of God, but rather points above all to Jesus and unites us with him to the Father.

The essence of Christianity is that faith, a joyful, grateful, rejoicing faith, stands at the forefront. 'Morality', the programme for one's life, does not come next, but gets its shape and life-force from faithful prayer and prayerful faith.

It would still be a misunderstanding to see faith, its wonder and gratitude, merely as the life-force and life's-blood of morality, be it even the sublime morality of love. The heaven that the Abba-prayer shows us does not consist in works, even the most magnificent, but rather in loving contemplation, wonder and gratitude, in rejoicing praise.

Praying in spirit and in truth is its own reward: all to the greater glory of God. The more we value prayer for itself, gathered closely around Jesus in the sight of the Father, the more we shall be changed from inside out, made into a new creation, and only then bear much fruit in love, goodness, but also in peacemaking love, in the service of the messianic call of peace.

Prayer and mission

The powerful words that rang out from heaven at Jesus' baptism: 'you are my beloved Son', are a dialogue of love, which entitled Jesus uniquely to call the Almighty God his 'Abba'. His last words, 'Abba, into your hands I commend my spirit' are the final answer, and at the same time the gate into majesty, in which Jesus is completely taken up in the inner essential dialogue of the triune God.

But between the call that empowered and acknowledged Jesus at his baptism in the Jordan, and the cry to 'Abba' at his homecoming, lies the mission of Jesus. Prayer and mission form a unique synthesis in Jesus' life. Part of our integrated life's programme is to understand this better, or at least to sense it.

Jesus prayed in private, but also in front of his disciples. Hearing his cry, 'Abba', in the Holy Spirit, seeing his countenance radiant with the glow of joyous love, was the high-point of their lives, and setting this example was an inseparable part of his mission to guide us, his disciples, in our integrated call in faith, prayer, love and the work of love, including the love of our enemies.

The public life of Jesus is bracketed by the powerful voice from heaven, of the Father: 'you are my beloved Son', and the last Abba-prayer of Jesus on the cross. It is the heart of his call and mission, to take us up into the love of the Father and of humanity, indeed of the whole creation. His coming from the Father and his going home to the Father are part of the eternal mystery of the triune God, but are also the heart of creation and the history of the world.

Christian prayer in the name of Jesus and with Jesus is always an assent to our mission, the realisation of the love of God for humanity and creation. What is decisive in this is faith, our abiding and our anchoring in the love of Jesus for the Father and for us, and thus in the love of the Father himself, through the power of the Holy Spirit. The more and the more vividly we let ourselves be taken into the dialogue that the Father initiates with his words: 'you are my beloved Son', and Jesus responds to with the final 'Abba!' on the cross, the more we open ourselves to our mission in the world and for the world. Prayer is the exact opposite of flight from the world and alienation from other people.

Profession of faith as worship and praise

The *Our Father* is a condensed profession of faith, which Jesus lived out and which instructs us. Only in worship and praise can we acknowledge faith in God, who is love in person. It is at the same time a commitment to acknowledge, honour and glorify God, who has revealed himself as love in the whole of our lives, above all in the realisation of his loving, caring, healing and forgiving love for all humanity.

Faith in the fullest sense is not just saying and expressing all that we hold to be true. Faith means, more ultimately, securing oneself in God, to love and honour him in thought, word and deed as our one and all.

When we pray the *Our Father* with our whole hearts, faith and life, religion and morality become an inseparable synthesis. In the communion of saints, united with Jesus, we commit ourselves – always trusting God's grace – to root our faith so deeply in our hearts, that he can shape all our senses and endeavours and also our action.

The Our Father *is trinitarian*

Our prayer is always connected to our baptism. This in turn must be understood in the light of Jesus' baptism. Jesus' baptism in the Jordan forms a whole with the baptism of Jesus in the Holy Spirit and in his blood.

Jesus sees the descent of the Holy Spirit in the form of a dove of peace. He knows that the Father has named him the beloved Son, on whom all his favour rests. In everything he says, proclaims and does, his is filled with the consciousness that 'the Spirit of the Lord rests on me, he has anointed me' *(Luke 4:16)*. In the Holy Spirit, in the breath of the love of the Father he rejoices 'Abba, Father' *(Luke 10:21)*. In the power of the Holy Spirit he consecrates himself and is consecrated by the Father for the salvation of the world.

When we make the sign of the cross or pray the *Our Father*, we do it in the light of Jesus' baptism and our communion with Jesus by the power of our baptism in the name of the triune God. We dare to use the unprecedented, bold address 'Abba, Abbuni', 'Father, our Father', because we know we are united with Jesus, gifted and sanctified through his Spirit.

The *Our Father* only really becomes the basic form of our faith and the same time our whole life's programme insofar as we consciously, gratefully and trustingly are aware of the trinitarian dimension of our Christian being, our faith and prayer.

Only in union with Jesus and animated and graced by his Holy Spirit do we enter into prayer and live before the countenance of Jesus' Abba, our Abba.

The trinitarian dimension of our prayer makes it an event that already contains a foretaste of heaven.

The whole of our life's programme

The whole of our life's programme and our call are contained in this double commandment: to love God with our whole heart and, united with Jesus and the Father in the power of the divine breath of love, to love our neighbour, not least the poor.

The first part of the *Our Father*, 'Hallowed be Thy name', is summed up in the bold, loving 'Thou'† we address to God, who has revealed himself to us as love. It is a joyful 'thank you' to be allowed to address, love and praise the Almighty intimately as our Father, as 'Thou'†.

It is the vow to test all our reflection, striving and action by whether and how seriously we take the name of the Father and our call as his sons and daughters, and honour it. Not least, we are confronted here above all with our mission to honour the one God and Father, to further peace and the solidarity of salvation for all people.

Careful reflection on Jesus' preaching of the Kingdom of God makes the love and worship of the Father concrete. Day by day, challenges and opportunities present themselves to testify to the Kingdom of God as the Kingdom of love and justice, of

---

† Translator's note: in German, as in the English of the past, 'thou' and not 'you' is the intimate address reserved for those to whom we are particularly close.

humility and reconciliation. How do we make it evident to people that our thinking, speaking, action are all about the Kingdom of love of God and neighbour which Christ proclaimed and made visible? God revealed his inexhaustible, glorious plan of salvation (his will) to us in his beloved Son.

We cannot pray for his will to be done day by day without constantly trying to mediate on and discover God's plan of salvation in the signs of the times. In doing so we are continually examining how seriously we take God's plan of salvation, seeking to understand it and acknowledging it in practice. It is an essential feature of our self-commitment, made in the power of the Holy Spirit, and always in the light of the beloved Son, to love God in all and above all and to fulfil his holy will of love.

The second part of the *Our Father* is about loving your neighbour along with Jesus. It is about us, the radical common life of Jesus' solidarity of salvation with all people in all spheres of life.

Just as the baptism of Jesus in the river Jordan was a trinitarian event, praying the *Our Father* takes us into the trinitarian life of God. Keeping this in mind, together with our fundamental option for the solidarity of salvation in all aspects of life, will doubtless help us to make our life's programme clearer and clearer, with more convincing contours.

2: Father in Heaven, hallowed be Thy Name

'Father, I have revealed your name…'

'LOVING FATHER, the world has not known you, but I have known you, and they have known that you sent me. I have made your name known to them and will make it known, so that the love with which you loved me is in them and that I might be in them' *(John 17:5-6; 2-26)*.

The question of the name of God is a fundamental question for all religious people, especially those however who receive and uphold the revelation of the Old and New Testaments.

The name of God which the patriarchs shared with their culture were above all El, Elohim, El-Shaddai; the names of the God of the Desert, who inspires terror with storms and terrifying events, but also sends blessings and fruitfulness. They are the names of the Unpredictable, the Unapproachable, but also the Bestower of Blessings, on whom all depend.

The revelation of the divine name Yahweh is one of the great and solemn events of the Old Testament. Moses said to God: 'when I go to the Israelites and say to them, "the God of your fathers has sent me to you" and they then ask me, "what is his name?" What shall I answer them?' And God said to Moses: 'I am who I am!' And he continued: 'you shall say to the Israelites: "Yahweh, the I-am-there, the God of your fathers, the God of Abraham, Isaac and Jacob has sent me to you. This is my name for evermore" ' *(Exodus 3:13-15)*.

He is the 'God of your fathers', the God of salvation-history, the God who chose, led and protected Abraham and his descendants. In contrast to the names they inherited for God, this is something new: the presence of God to his persecuted people, his protecting and liberating presence. The people honour him in placing all their trust in him, in his name, walking in his ways, remaining true to his covenant. Yahweh himself proclaims this solemnly, in saying of himself: 'Yahweh, Yahweh, a gracious and merciful God, slow to anger and rich in grace and fidelity' *(Exodus 34:6)*. There is no other God besides Yahweh. Honouring his name is the commandment above all others: 'thou shalt not worship any other God; "Jealous One" is the name of Yahweh, and he is a jealous God' *(Exodus 34:14)*.

The divine name Yahweh is the expression of fatherly care, presence, liberating power, but also an expression of holiness – 'God in Heaven'. He desires reverence. God will not let his name be misused for ungodly acts or thoughts. 'Thou shalt not take the name of Yahweh your God in vain; for Yahweh will not let those who misuse his name for evil-doing go unpunished' *(Deuteronomy 5:11)*.

But in the end the honour of the name of God is not about mere prohibitions, not even about the many individual commandments. Yahweh declaims solemnly what the crux of honour is, what he expects from his people, his chosen ones: 'hear, O Israel, "I-am-there" (Yahweh), our God is the only "I-am-there" (Yahweh)! You shall love Yahweh your God with your whole heart, your whole soul, and with all your power! And these words which I command you shall remain in your heart' *(Deuteronomy 6:4-6)*. It is a question of all-encompassing love and a thankful mind and heart.

The unprecedented novelty of calling God 'Abba'

We Christians cannot marvel enough and be grateful enough for Jesus' revelation of the name Abba. The way in which Jesus extols the name 'Abba' for God is unheard-of and unsurpassable.

The peak of the experience of the loving, saving and liberating presence of God is already expressed in the promise of Jesus' title 'Emmanuel', 'God-with-us'. 'El', the name of God that expresses his supremacy, is united with 'presence' in Jesus, in his own religious experience and in his whole life and testimony to this unique presence. The Father's word made human is supremacy in humility, in the charm of the child in the crib, in the heartfelt love of Jesus for the Father and for humanity. In a religious world that is entirely characterised by the divine names of El-Shaddai, Elohim, the revelation of God in Jesus is simply unthinkable. It surpasses all our categories of thought. Here there can only be astonishment, gratitude, faith, humble adoration.

The fundamental experience of presence, of tender love

Jesus is true God, Emmanuel – God with us, but also true man, with real human experience and development. The experience that conditioned the psychic life of Jesus is the tender love of his mother and his adoptive father Joseph. The child Jesus expressed this experience with two nick-names: IMMA (Mamma) and ABBA (Papa, dear father). There was and is no child so worthy of love and so beloved as Jesus. Even more: there is no child who reciprocated the love he received so purely and strongly as Jesus, and expressed it in the names IMMA and ABBA.

This is combined with Jesus' religious experience which was a gift of absolute grace, that surpasses all mystical experience of all people: the experience that his IMMA (Mary) and his ABBA (Joseph) were images, reflections of the maternal-paternal love of the heavenly Father. Jesus increased in age and wisdom and the grace of God *(Luke 2:52)*. He knows with all his human faculties that he comes from the Father and that a quite special love comes to him as the Son of God. In a unique way, he may call the Almighty ABBA. He may invite his disciples and all that believe in him to call Yahweh ABBA along with him: 'my Father and your Father' *(John 20:17)*.

Jesus' total being-for-God, the Lord of heaven and earth, and Jesus' total being-for-us human beings peaks in the revelation of the name 'ABBA' for Yahweh. When Jesus before his death prays in his great ABBA-prayer: 'I have revealed your name to those you have given me from the world. They were yours and you have given them to me' *(John 17:6)*, it is a cry of joy and thanks. That does not only mean that he tells us, his disciples, the name which he uses for the Father and which glorifies him. Much more: his whole being for the Almighty, who is Presence and Love, and his entire mission for us human beings, make the Father visible. 'Whoever has seen me, has seen ABBA' *(John 14:9)*.

All the biblical texts in which Jesus calls God, the Almighty, ABBA, are keys that help us to know and understand the Father in heaven, as we may, can, and must honour, love, and glorify the name of the Father.

Rejoicing in the Holy Breath

The hour when the disciples, these simple, humble men, came back from their first journey of preaching and joyfully related their experiences of faith, was a unique hour of grace for the revelation of the name of God: 'in that hour of grace Jesus rejoiced in the Holy Breath and spoke full of joy: I praise you, ABBA, Lord of heaven and earth, for revealing to little ones what was concealed from the learned. Yes, ABBA, that is what pleased you to do. All has been confided to me by my ABBA; no one knows the Son except the Father and no one knows the Father except the Son and those to whom the Son has revealed it' *(Luke 10:21-22)*.

This is a trinitarian prayer through and through, a prayer that is itself trinitarian praise. I am deliberately translating the usual word that corresponds to *Spirit* in the Hebrew and the Greek (*ruach* and *pneuma*) with *Breath*. The Holy BREATH is the primal, eternal event of the love that gives itself and is given back between Father and Son. It is the Breath of love and life as much of the Father as of the Son. This event in timeless heaven becomes a saving event on earth, first in Jesus, and then in his disciples. How happily must Mary, his mother, have marvelled, as she realised that her Son, Jesus, called the 'Lord of heaven and earth' his ABBA! To Jesus, who had made himself the least, the Almighty had revealed himself 'on earth' as a loving ABBA. It is Jesus' joy, the reason for exulting in the BREATH of love, that God in heaven has revealed himself on earth as ABBA.

The cry of ABBA and all that Jesus experienced before us teaches us that we must become small before God, humble before our fellow human beings, to be taken up into the eternal cry of ABBA.

'God is humility'. That is how Sr Celeste Crosta-rosa, the founder of the Order of the Redemptorists, experienced it. Therefore the meeting-place with the Almighty, the Lord God of heaven and earth, is our nothingness, the consciousness that we have been called by God out of nothing and stand before him with paltry works and qualities. The more humbly and gratefully we praise God for revealing these things to the lowly, the more we already sense in earthly life something of the bliss of Jesus' joyful cry of 'ABBA-Father'.

Jesus is the epitome of the worship of God in spirit and in truth. This can be seen just in the humility of the incomprehensible event of the incarnation of the word of God; but also through the humility of his whole life through to the humility of his 'death on a cross'.

Let us see how Jesus glorifies the all-holy and beloved name of the Father: he is completely absorbed in the proclamation of and witness to the kingdom of the love, grace, and peace of the Father: 'thy kingdom come.'

He is completely absorbed in the assent to the Father's plan of salvation to destroy the vicious circle of violence, falsehood, lust for power, and the ostentation of the sinful world. He committed himself to do this through his suffering as the humble, non-violent servant of God and by preparing the way of peace: 'thy will be done.'

'On earth as it is in heaven.' Heaven is the triune

God in its eternal celebration of love, in its eternal, overflowing love and in its eternal plan of salvation. In Jesus, and in turn in his disciples, this increasingly becomes an earthly event.

In a unique way, the name of God the Father is glorified on earth in the humiliation of the cross through his humble, non-violent Son and suffering Servant Jesus. This is condensed into the prayer of the crucified one: 'ABBA, forgive!'

In his bitter death-pangs, Jesus glorifies the heavenly ABBA on earth in his last prayer, his last BREATH of love: 'ABBA! into your hands I commend my BREATH.'

In his words and his whole life, but above all on the cross, Jesus glorifies the name of his ABBA by completely unmasking the 'satanic temptations' *(Matthew 4)*, the misuse of religion and the name of God for one's own profit, for unjust power over others, for sacralised display. 'Lead us not into temptation.'

In his whole work of redemption, Jesus sanctifies, reveals and glorifies God's name ABBA by conquering evil with good, hatred through his reconciling love (cf. 'Do not be overcome by evil, but overcome evil with good' *(Romans 12:21)* and 'Deliver us from evil').

Thus we see that the whole of the *Lord's Prayer* gives us the clearest indication of how we can honour, praise, love and glorify the name of God, our ABBA, in our living and striving, as individuals or communities.

Prayer

ABBA, our Father and Father of our Lord Jesus Christ, we praise you; for through your beloved Son you have made your fatherly name known and glorified from the rising of the sun to its setting.
We thank you for calling us, united with Jesus, to honour your fatherly name with a great trust in your goodness, with grateful love, with humility and boundless reverence.
Let the Holy Breath flow through us, the spirit of truth, that alone can teach us to 'worship you', the almighty God, 'in spirit and in truth'.
We thank you for letting us address you intimately in our hearts, as we unite ourselves completely with your beloved Son Jesus and participate in his loving longing to make your fatherly name known to all humanity and to be glorified in all things.

3: Thy Kingdom come

*'Jesus proclaimed the good news of God: the time
of grace is fulfilled, and the kingdom of God is
near: repent and believe in the Gospel.'*
(Mark 1:15)

THE THREE synoptic Gospels are above all the good
news of the Kingdom of God. Often it is called
the 'Kingdom of Heaven'. The biblical expression is
particularly significant: 'the Kingdom of the Father'.
The prayer in the *Our Father*, 'thy kingdom come',
refers unambiguously to the Kingdom of ABBA, the
Father of our Lord Jesus Christ and our Father.
Following this, it can always be translated: 'the
Father's reign of love'. The address *Our Father* alone,
which resonates throughout the whole of the *Lord's
Prayer*, makes it clear that it is a reign of love. The
Kingdom of Heaven, the Kingdom of God, the
Kingdom of the Father of our Lord Jesus Christ is
the reign of the love of the Father whom Jesus loved
with his whole heart, who pressingly invites us to
enter into this very Kingdom. He invites us to en-
trust ourselves completely to the rule of God's love
and to submit ourselves to it and serve it.

Jesus' preaching of the Kingdom of the Father is
good news through and through, the precious mes-

sage of grace: receive the gift of the Father's bound-less love and grace! Let his love, his peace, his grace fill your hearts and shape your lives!

Let us go into the question which is so important to us: who may share in the Father's Kingdom? Who really does enter into this encompassing Kingdom of Grace?

Jesus gives a very clear answer in the *Beatitudes* in the Sermon on the Mount. All the *Beatitudes* are enveloped in the promise with which the first and last *Beatitudes* end: 'the Kingdom of Heaven is theirs'. Jesus himself is the epitome and the perfect embodiment of the *Beatitudes*. 'Blessed are those who are poor by the power of the (Holy) Spirit: theirs is the Kingdom of Heaven' *(Matthew 5:3)*. Jesus says, 'among all human beings there has been no one greater than John the Baptist. But the least in the Kingdom of Heaven is greater than he' *(Matthew 11:11)*. Jesus himself is the one who is 'in the King-dom of Heaven', in the Kingdom of his Father, who has made himself the least: he is all receptivity, all humility, all gratitude. Even in his humanity he is completely taken up in the breath of love (the 'Holy Breath'), in which the Father gives himself to the Son and Son to the Father.

To know oneself as given, to always allow oneself to be given, without holding back something for oneself – that is the great *Beatitude*.

In his whole being, in his baptism, in his life, in the washing of the feet, in the abandonment on the cross, Jesus embodies the first and last *Beatitude*. The Father has given the Kingdom to him, the humble 'servant of God'. In the Kingdom of Christ and the Father there is no ostentation, no fighting for higher rank. He, who before his death performed the most humble service, promises those who follow him in it: 'therefore I confer the Kingdom on you, as the Father has conferred it on me' *(Luke 22:29)*.

Whoever does not set themselves free from the 'works of deep-rooted selfishness ... will not inherit the Kingdom of God' *(Galatians 5:21)*. It belongs to those who 'produce the fruits of the Spirit: love, joy, peace, forbearance, friendliness, goodness, fidelity, non-violence and self-control' *(Galatians 15:22)*. They share in the Kingdom of the Father and Christ.

The 'Kingdom of the Father' is utterly different from the 'Kingdom of this world' with its struggles for power, its solemn titles of honour, its ostentation, its lack of peace and lust for war.

Therefore it takes a radical conversion, a radical re-thinking, to let oneself be embraced, given and led by the Kingdom of the Father. The proclamation of the Kingdom of God and likewise our prayer for the coming of the Kingdom of God are a grand offer from God. They are at once liberating and healing, but also a warning against any relapse into what is perverted and trivial. 'The Kingdom of God is not eating and drinking' or indeed intolerant fighting over such things, 'rather justice, peace and joy in the Holy

31

Spirit' *(Romans 14:17)*. 'Whoever serves Christ in this way is recognised by God and despised by human beings' *(Romans 14:18)*. This refers to our exalted calling as witnesses to the Kingdom of God. Those who are called marvel in gratitude: the Father 'has snatched them out of the kingdom of darkness and has planted them in the Kingdom of his beloved Son' *(Colossians 1:13)*. Those who live according to this calling, 'these are good seed, sons and daughters of the Kingdom' *(Matthew 13:38)*.

The parables of the Kingdom of God

The parables of the Kingdom of God are countless, particularly in the Gospel of Matthew. In their entirety they give us an outline of the Kingdom of God and say what we can and should do to pray honestly for the coming of the Kingdom of God and hope to be heard.

The parable of the sower
(Matthew 13:19; Mark 4:1-9)

The good news that the divine sower proclaims by his example and word is accompanied by the works of grace of the Holy Spirit. But in the end it also depends on us human beings, that like Mary, the mother of Jesus, we do not just hear it in a superficial way, but take it gratefully into our hearts, preserve it in a grateful mind and do everything possible to put it into practice. We ourselves should become fruitful seeds of the Kingdom of God. But first of all our task is to prepare the ground, to become a good, fertile soil for the precious seed.

The parable of the mustard seed and the dough
(Matthew 13:31-33)

The Kingdom of God comes to us in the power of the love of God, that has been made visible for us in Christ. But it requires a long and difficult process of germination and growth. After the first decisive repentance our whole life must become a continuing repentance, deepening and purification, so that the message of the Kingdom of God bears much fruit in us and through us. We need forbearance and patience, but above all a constantly growing fidelity and vigilance.

We must believe that we are capable of great things, for God has great things in store for us and is always anticipating us with his grace. But we must not let ourselves be overtaken by impatience and act at the wrong time. Above all, let us not focus these precious powers on what is of secondary importance and try to force results at an inopportune moment.

We should mutually encourage one another. That presupposes that each of us abstains from trivial criticism and does not put pressure on one another. Only the power of selfless love liberates, heals and inspires.

The parables of the treasure and of the pearl
(Matthew 13:44-46)

Whatever costly treasures are unearthed from Pharaoh's tombs or anywhere else are trivialities compared to the utterly priceless wealth of our call to the Kingdom of the Father, and not only as ones who receive the most magnificent gifts, but also as honoured fellow-workers on the field of the Kingdom of God. The man who sells everything to gain the field in which a valuable treasure is buried, and the man who sells everything to buy a precious pearl should motivate us to follow our exalted vocation to bear fruit for the Kingdom of God, to be and to become 'sons and daughters of the Kingdom of God' more and more, to prize God's Kingdom and care for it above all. The parables show us the conviction that is also embodied in the self-abandonment of Jesus unto death on the cross. This conviction should combine all our energies and enthusiasm in prayer for the coming of the Kingdom of God and in a lifestyle and a way of acting that shows our prayer to be authentic. It also requires constant vigilance that we do not pass up any precious opportunity to serve the coming of the Kingdom of God in ourselves and in others.

'On earth as it is in heaven'

The Kingdom of Heaven, the Kingdom of the Father and the beloved Son, is anticipated in the triune life of God, in the eternal primal event of the self-giving love between Father and Son in the eternal BREATH of love. It appeared on earth in Jesus. It radiates wonderfully from the Holy Family and in the community of disciples, above all after the event of Pentecost. We number the community of saints among those in the heavenly Kingdom of God, who are forever with God, in the majesty of God. This heavenly sphere is prepared for all who long vividly for heaven, for the full participation in the Kingdom of the Father and the beloved Son. And this should be an incentive to pray more ardently for the coming of the Kingdom of God on earth and to continually discover anew what we can do in this respect.

The horizon that is expressed in the phrase 'on earth as it is in heaven', warns us against becoming arrested in the earthly and also against narrow-mindedness and restriction in our efforts for the coming of the Kingdom of God.

The phrase, 'on earth as it is in heaven' expresses a crucial dimension of our fundamental decision for the Kingdom of the Father and his beloved Son. We should never slacken in our own progressive repentance as well as in our efforts for the cultivation of the earthly Kingdom of God. Our fundamental decision for the solidarity of salvation and the corresponding prayer must continually deepen and take shape in our whole life.

The Church and the Kingdom of God

The Church is not the Kingdom of God. It is called to become the servant, proclaimer, and 'sacrament' of the Kingdom of God. All triumphalism, every form of self-justification contradicts the dimension which is expressed in the phrase 'on earth as it is in heaven'. The Church – and indeed we are all the Church – must not preach itself. It may not cling to any assets. Only as a pilgrim Church is it an effective witness to the coming of the Kingdom of God 'on earth as it is in heaven'. On earth as in the life of the Church it will never be as simple as it is in heaven. But we must continually measure ourselves against this dynamic of being on the way to the heavenly Kingdom.

The Church in its offices, its structures, its theology, and in its office-holders is only holy to the degree that it is a penitent: confessing its failure to live up to its call, not indulging in fruitless apologetic and singing its own praises; confessing to mistakes where they exist and making its way along new paths.

The prayer 'thy Kingdom come, on earth as it is in heaven' awakens in us a healing restlessness; it is an ongoing incentive and motivation. The prayer warns us however against despondency and pessimism. We have the attitude of a pilgrim Church, and do not settle in any resting place, but struggle to our feet to make new departures, to act in accordance with our prayer for the coming of the Kingdom of God.

Prayer

Almighty God and Father, in praying for the coming of your Kingdom I am sometimes very frightened. I must ask myself whether I have always meant it when I prayed for the coming of your reign of love. Otherwise how could trivial things shatter my peace as if they were more important than the revelation of your Kingdom of love, justice and peace. I must truly be ashamed of myself. And yet I dare, trusting in your grace, to pray for this all-encompassing fundamental request. Yes, I ask you for the grace of total determination, to seek in future first the Kingdom of your love in all and above all. Give me the courage to see the inevitable consequences of this prayer and to live accordingly. If I did not know from your beloved Son that your divine patience and forbearance also are part of the coming of your Kingdom, I would not dare to say this bold prayer.

4: Thy will be done on earth as it is in heaven

'Not everyone who says to me "Lord! Lord!" will enter into the Kingdom of heaven, but only those who do the will of my Father.'
(Matthew 7:21)

'Whoever does the will of my Father is my brother, sister, and mother.'
(Matthew 12:50; Mark 3:35)

'My mother and my brothers and sisters are those who hear the word of God and do it.'
(Luke 8:21)

JUST AS one can translate 'the Kingdom of God' as the reign of love of the Father, so in the third petition of the *Our Father* the word *thelema*, that is usually translated as *will*, can mean *the will of love*. In most contexts in the New Testament it means God's plan of salvation. So we can pray: 'your loving will be done' or 'may your plan of salvation be fulfilled'!

Before his suffering, with exactly the same words as in the third petition of the *Our Father*, Jesus expressed his committed assent to the Father's plan of salvation, whose crux is Jesus' mission as the non-violent suffering Servant and Son of God.

The Greek word *thelema* in no way means a sheer willing or a stern imposition. It is instead the will of ABBA, the kindly Father. It always refers to God's whole plan of salvation, our Father's, who is fulfilled in Jesus Christ. We pray for his saving will, the saving plan of God, revealed in Jesus and fulfilled to the end. 'In heaven', in the heart of the triune God, in the eternal divine primal event of the self-giving mutual love of the Father and the Son in the Breath of love, there is no sheer willing, still less a tyrannical will.

The lure of love

Neither the Father nor Jesus force their will on us. In God's plan of salvation, in his loving will, love always acts as a lure, an invitation to the eternal celebration of love. We are never slaves to God's plan of salvation, but rather 'sons and daughters of the Kingdom', who, together with the beloved Son, are called to work together in freedom and for freedom in the Kingdom of love and peace.

This lure of love is expressed in an unsurpassable form in Jesus' response, when he was told that his mother and brothers and sisters were standing outside and wanted to speak to him. He stretched out his arms and promised something unbelievably beautiful to us, his disciples, who pray for the fulfilment of God's plan of salvation for and through ourselves: 'when you say "Yes" to the loving will of my ABBA with your heart and your will and in your whole life, then you will be as dear to me as brothers and sisters, yes even my mother!' There is nothing higher than this. We would have to have a heart of stone not to be deeply moved by this, the Saviour's lure of love; not to allow ourselves to be enticed. And that means setting oneself decisively on the way to complete trust in the loving will of God, in seeking first to understand in everything what the loving will of God wants from us here and now.

Conformity with the loving will of God

St Alphonsus summed up his entire spirituality, indeed his whole Christian moral theology with the expression: 'conformity with the loving will of God'. By this he basically meant the same thing as Meister Eckhart and Henry Suso did in their formula 'Letting-be'.

This rests on the rock-firm faith that God is love, and consequently 'what God does is well done.' The heart of the ABBA-prayer is to abide in God's holy will. We can accomplish it only in union with Jesus and in the power of the LOVING BREATH (the Holy Spirit), who is the eternal joyful primal event of the self-giving mutual love between the Father and the Son.

Conformity with the will of God is an expression of rock-firm trust in God's love, the unshakeable

41

confidence that God's plan of salvation is for the best and that it will be fulfilled when we abide in God in thought, word, and deed. In the meantime we do whatever is possible to recognize God's will concretely, and act or suffer accordingly.

That is a great grace, a great chain or a great river of grace. And that is precisely why we pray: 'thy will be done on earth as it is in heaven.'

We know from the word of God and the example of Christ and his saints that the heart of the matter is 'purity of heart', pure thoughts, seeking God's will in all things, seeking to please God in all things.

How do we recognise God's will?

To recognise God's will concretely in the present hour requires a deep insight of faith into God's plan of salvation, as it is made visible for us in Jesus Christ, his Son and our Redeemer. Jesus made the Father's loving will, his plan of salvation visible in all that he did and said, in his life and death. The non-violent, peacemaking love of God and his humble Servant-Son plays a crucial role in this.

The Father loved us first, while we were still sinners. Jesus shows us the way of peace. Through his absolute non-violence and his courageous witness for the truth he breaks the destructive chain of hate, enmity, revenge, bitterness.

Therefore a fundamental presupposition for an unerring recognition of God's will is the basic decision to follow Jesus in his peacemaking love and in union with all people of good will to serve peace and justice.

The trio 'peace, justice and preservation of creation' is certainly the gist of God's plan of salvation, as it bears on us today in the light of Jesus and the signs of the times.

In God's plan of salvation it is all about learning to love: learning to know and love Jesus, and then with Jesus to love the Father and all people. St Alphonsus, whose central idea is conformity with the loving will of God the Father, gives us an instruction in his book *Learning to love Jesus* (*Pratica di amar Gesù Christo*). He follows the magnificent picture that Paul paints in *1 Corinthians 13* of the true face of love; which is a redeemed and redeeming love, as it is visible in Jesus and as it is reflected in the many saints.

When we read in Paul that 'love is patient, love is kind ...' we do well to read between the lines, 'Jesus is patient, kind ...'

The lives of great and modest saints, including those who are still living among us, help us to apply what is eternal in the love of Jesus to current historical situations in a sensible way.

Is our suffering, even cruel suffering, God's will?

One thing is certain: God abhors the senseless suffering human beings do to one another. Jesus clearly shows that he would rather suffer the utmost himself than cause suffering to another, even his enemies. The Father's plan of salvation, as he fulfilled it, breaks the destructive chain of retribution and revenge.

The fearsome possibility that human beings can inflict senseless suffering and frightful pain on one another is only permitted indirectly by God, insofar as it is taken account of in his plan of salvation. The profound mystery of suffering with all its unfathomable dimensions is, so to speak, an unavoidable risk of the creation of free human beings. God created humanity to be free to do good. But with the unavoidable imperfection of creation – God cannot create God – there exists unfortunately the possibility that human beings could misuse their freedom for their own harm and to harm their fellow human beings. We can only think with horror to what extent people have misused their freedom to construct a whole chain of disasters and injustices. The worst evil in suffering of every kind is the consequence of sin, above all the fundamental choice by many of the chains of sin rather than, as God wanted, the solidarity of salvation.

The whole life, suffering and teaching of Jesus shows us the unambiguous way towards the solidarity of salvation, that can only break through the destructive chain of sin and suffering by power of Jesus' mediation. Above all, we can do this only by fulfilling his basic commandment and basic plan: 'each bears one another's burdens, and thus you will fulfil the law of Christ' *(Galatians 6:2)*.

To our fellow human beings, who are deeply wounded by heavy suffering and disappointments and are often tempted to go astray from God's plan of salvation, I used to say and write quite concretely: 'it was certainly not God who ordained that I should have cancer and that I should have a relapse.' In God I see above all the source of grace and of light, that makes it possible for me to cope with these and other sufferings meaningfully, with a grateful glance at the suffering and patience of Jesus and his saints.

Let us stay with the example of cancer for a moment. It can have many proximate causes: eg. smoking (I myself was never a smoker). Very often living with a heavy smoker plays a not insignificant role, among others, like weakened health which may be culpable or in no way culpable, bitter suffering and injustices inflicted by others that one never came to terms with, perhaps also because those concerned have not yet reached that level of tolerance and conformity with God's plan of salvation that could have proved itself to be a source of health.

We must be very careful about talk of 'suffering in expiation'. Any form of thinking or speaking that ascribes to God an 'avenging justice' must be absolutely avoided. God does not avenge himself. But sin, above all remaining in the solidarity of doom, can 'avenge itself'. Even where masses of sins and sinful structures 'vengefully' strike back, we can and should direct our gaze and our heart to the healing and forgiving love of God, who does not want death, but repentance and salvation. He wants to turn every kind of suffering to the good in his plan of salvation, above all bitter suffering that is senselessly inflicted on us by others, but also the consequences of our own sins – assuming that we are prepared to co-operate with this.

In suffering of every kind we can learn compassion, above all, and in this respect be like Jesus and the heavenly Father, of whom Jesus said: 'Be full of compassion, because your heavenly Father is also full of compassion' *(Luke 6:36)*. Suffering is transformed, it becomes fruitful, when it helps us to grow deeper into God's plan of salvation, when our love for God and neighbour is purified in the furnace of suffering. Suffering born meaningfully can become a precious witness for the merciful love of God for us human beings.

Above all it should be emphasised that in no case should we set forth profound theories on the meaning and/or meaninglessness of suffering, so long as we have not done all that we can to prevent unnecessary suffering, heal curable diseases so far as possible, fight against the injustices that senseless suffering produces.

It is also part of our assent without reserve or conditions to the loving will of God that we untiringly strive to understand it better and act accordingly, but finally to also humbly acknowledge our limits in the interpretation of it, our partial impotence with respect to cruel suffering.

The virtue of criticism of the Church and the world

A disastrous source of many sufferings and even loss of faith was and is the radical renunciation of the virtue of criticism of the real Church. Connected to this, and partly a consequence of it, are false obedience and uncritical acceptance of sinful structures in the secular world as well, sometimes to the point of executing criminal orders.

If men of the Church in the higher and highest ranks demand uncritical and absolute obedience to their will, and do so in the name of God, then before they pray the *Our Father* and 'thy will be done', they must thoroughly test whether they might have refused to double-check carefully, in solidarity with the community of faith and other competent people, whether their will is really an expression of God's plan of salvation and the Gospel.

Harsh commands and prohibitions and demands for conformity and forbidding proper criticism of truths that are not revealed can amount to a kind of polytheism, if they pray 'thy will be done', yet demand uncritical obedience in the name of God, perhaps placing greater emphasis on this than on the real truths and demands of the Gospel. In practice, if we always require uncritical acceptance of our instructions or teachings, we must all test our consciences very carefully to whether we might have substituted our own will for God's will.

Our prayer for the fulfilment of the will of God can only be realistic and true to life within a humble community of learning in which we all help one another to recognise God's will in the concrete. We must help one another and let ourselves be helped to arrive at the best possible knowledge of God's plan of salvation and a meaningful interpretation of the signs of the times.

Our prayer for God's help in fulfilling his plan of salvation in us and through us includes praying for the grace of persistence in doing the will of God. In this petition of the *Our Father* we pray not least for the special grace to be able to pray together with Jesus in the face of death and the pains of death: 'Father, let your will, not mine, be done!'

We can long for and pray for no greater grace, than that in the hour of death our will might be entirely united with the loving will of God.

Prayer

*Father, your beloved Son Jesus Christ has made
known to us and taught us not only your wonderful
plan of salvation, and confided to us your whole
will of love. He has made us see the mighty power
of this prayer 'thy will be done' through his prayer
in the face of death down to the last breath. He has
shown us that we truly are free forever, if we give
ourselves over to you and your holy will completely.
Again and again, when I say this fundamental
prayer 'thy will be done' aloud and in my heart, the
nervous question comes up as to whether I am really
saying it in all honesty.*

*I fear that my own will might always be playing
tricks on me. Give us all the courage, together with
the virtue of discernment, to cultivate authentic
criticism, so that we might all come to seek only
your will and also understand unerringly what you
expect from us.*

*Forgive me graciously for so often saying this
prayer thoughtlessly or superficially, without
seeking to make the loving knowledge of your will
the heart of the matter.*

5: Give us this day our daily bread

*'Then the disciples said to one another: has
someone been bringing him something to eat?
Jesus said to them: "my precious food is to do the
will of the one who sent me, and to complete his
work of salvation." '*

(John 4:34)

THIS WONDERFUL text says something to us about
the link between the assent to God's will of salvation and the petition for bread. Only when we have
acquired the taste for investigating the plan of salvation and doing the will of God, like Jesus, will we
gradually understand how wonderfully God nourishes us through the word of good news, through
the Eucharistic bread, but also through daily bread.

My bread or our bread?

In the first three petitions of the *Our Father*, we
stand before our heavenly Father, who is incomprehensible and yet in his infinite love so near to us.
Insignificant though we are, he has called us to wonderful things, and only before him and through him
do we find our true selves, our real names.

In prayer we must never forget that we are always included in the great family of God, the community of salvation. No man is an island. Only united with Jesus and all his sisters and brothers do we dare to say, *Our Father*! He is the Father of our Lord Jesus Christ and the Father of all who belong to Christ.

We must never forget that the holy BREATH that goes out from the Father and the Son unites us with Christ and with all who belong to him. He takes us up into the heavenly world of God, the Father and the Son and all his saints and angels. In faith we find ourselves always lifted up into the all-encompassing community of salvation, the heavenly table fellowship.

We only truly think in terms of 'we'/'us', when our concern really is for bread for all, for reconciliation and peace for all, the victory over sin and temptation. Here on earth we struggle in solidarity against all the powers of doom, for it is a question of the salvation of all in the sight of Jesus, who calls himself the 'bread of life' *(John 6:55)*. He is the great gift of the Father to all, 'the bread that has come down from heaven' *(John 6:41)*.

Knowing that we pray united with Jesus, it is also clear to us that concern for our daily bread is only meaningful and sensible insofar as it means being nourished and living on the word 'that comes from the mouth of God' *(Matthew 4)*.

Through the promise of the heavenly banquet of

love and bliss and the Eucharistic feast of love, Jesus makes it absolutely clear to us that we may not come with him before the Father as long as each of us is only concerned with 'his' and/or 'my' bread. Bread symbolically stands for all earthly gifts.

What is crucial in relation to bread and all that is earthly is whether we honour it as a gift of the one Father, in order to feel ourselves bound to one another and the one Father, or whether we become prisoners of our selfishness, incurable squabblers in a murderous conflict over 'my bread' and 'your bread'.

If we would honour one another and all that we have and do as gifts of the one heavenly Father, then our bread would never run out, but better still, then we would somehow be in Paradise once again.

I would want to interpret the fall in this way: the gifts of the one Father, 'our bread', is turned by selfishness into 'my bread', my self-seeking, my seeking for domination. Our bread given to us in solidarity from God, is turned into a continual object of struggle, a medium of exploitation and demarcation.

The Eucharistic transformation of bread and wine into the body and blood of Christ is absolutely incomprehensible for our limited understanding. But we can approach the mystery to a certain extent when we reflect what a magnificent 'transformation' of our whole being and being together could take place, if we could honour all our bread and all else radically as a gift of the one Father. Then and only then would we leave behind us asinine fighting and bestow love on one another richly, to the honour of the one Father.

Gift of the one Father or 'my benefit'?

As soon as people, singly and collectively, forget thanks and above all cease to thank God through their whole conduct, then the right of the strongest, the insistence on one's own benefit holds sway! Every selfish inclination with a demand for one's own benefit leads to dispossession of another and to one's own radical estrangement. The consequences of selfish inclinations, in denying that our being before God is a gift, leads to fatal rivalry, to jealousy of someone else's position, rapacity, enmity, violence. Not only are things and situations desecrated by this, but the human person itself, who is degraded to the prisoner of his own selfishness, is alienated, desecrated, besmirched.

People who pray honestly and truly, 'Father, give us today our daily bread!' Return home to their Father's house, become free from the sinister compulsion of slavery to pile up more and more goods for oneself to the detriment of others. They become instead peace-loving, non-violent, concerned about solidarity. We cannot reflect enough upon this miracle of the transformation of earthly goods back into their true status as gifts of our shared heavenly Father.

Then the Kingdom of the Father, the Kingdom of peace and of love truly begins. This occurs wherever a community of people seriously begins to seek its precious nourishment in God's Kingdom, and to act in daily life according to God's plan of salvation in the sphere of economy, society, and politics. And that means, not least, to honour oneself with all one's abilities and also all earthly goods as gifts of the one God.

If one overlooks this dimension of the transformation of earthly things that are given to us, then one will hardly gain access to other spheres of life that are described in the Gospel by the symbolic term 'bread': the bread of the life-giving word of God, the Eucharistic meal and finally Christ in person, who calls himself the 'bread of life'.

The bread of life to the glory of God

What comes 'from below' discloses the vision 'from above'. Let us always reflect in wonder, gratitude and faith that Jesus was sent to us by the Father to become 'one of us', to surrender himself radically for us as the 'bread of life', is there for us, lives, dies and rises again. As according to God's plan of salvation the bread is there for all, to nourish and unite all, so too is Jesus the all-encompassing gift of the one Father for all humanity, to call us all to unity.

Christ is the solidarity of salvation in person. In this light, roughly and gradually, we can understand the doctrine of redemption and original sin. If one nonsensically sees original sin just as a blemish on the soul of the new-born baby that has to be washed away by baptism as quickly as possible, one has made the mystery of redemption and original entanglement in sin trivial and unbelievable. The truth is infinitely greater, richer, more beautiful, perhaps also more challenging.

Are we really monotheists?

It was long debated in the Church whether the teaching on original sin, rightly understood, necessarily presupposes monogenism, that is the assertion that all human beings have descended from a single human couple, as it appears in the biblical story of Adam and Eve.

Today in theology we know that much more is involved, namely the question of true monotheism, that is the belief in one God and Creator. This is part of the comprehensive vision of the solidarity of salvation or doom, which is the core of the teaching of redemption and original sin. The triune God, Father, Son and Holy Spirit as the ONE created the ALL, from inner freedom. But since he is truly the ONE, his creation from inner necessity is correlated to oneness, solidarity.

The ALL, which is created by his word, is entirely related to him, dependent on him, exists for his glory. All creatures gifted with reason and freedom are therefore enfolded by a mysterious solidarity of salvation. However, if some of the creatures gifted with freedom cast aside freedom as a gift and grab at their own lordliness, then the solidarity of salvation has its sinister shadow-side as a solidarity of doom. The usurpation of freedom is also at the same time a rejection of the solidarity of salvation. Because this solidarity only comes from God, this rebellious history of freedom itself becomes the solidarity of doom, not so much because of a single original set of parents, but rather just because of the primal fact of monotheism. In all decay, whatever rejects solidarity in and for God is marked out by the refusal of the solidarity of salvation. And this is precisely the hard core of the solidarity of doom, the reciprocal enslavement and enchainment in doom. The rebel is more and more tangled up in reciprocal enslavement.

Jesus, 'the bread of life', wholly a gift of the Father, wholly given to the Father and to humanity, is the solidarity of salvation in person, the Redeemer and redemption. He is free being-for-the-other. As the non-violent servant of God acknowledged by the Father as his beloved Son, he throws himself into the breach for all. He consecrates himself therefore in the River Jordan for the honour of the one God and Father. 'By his wounds we are healed' *(Isaiah 53:5)*. All are called to turn back and return home to him and through him to the Father. That is the crux of our understanding of baptism. Without a free return to the solidarity of salvation in Christ there is no liberation from the solidarity of doom (original sin).

The claim that the innocent child comes into the world with an inherited burden is not a statement that is sufficient in itself. The fundamental point is rather that the child is born according to God's plan of salvation into a world that is thoroughly stamped with the solidarity of salvation in Christ. Everything good from the past – always with Christ in the centre – is so to speak an original grace in our whole history. This original grace is spoken to us in visible signs in baptism and finally in faith. The ground of the source and goal are entirely stamped with the solidarity of salvation, from being for one another and with one another in Christ to the glory of God the Father.

In this respect it also becomes clear that no matter how horrible the solidarity of doom, the chain of sin, the unity in salvation in Christ for all who seek him is infinitely more powerful. It is incumbent then on each and every one of us to contribute to the solidarity of salvation becoming more clearly and strongly realised in historical reality and the environment.

A clear programme for life

Even in this great vision of the symbol of the bread, in whose centre is the radiant Christ, the prayer for bread also has much to say to us about the *Our Father* being a comprehensive life-programme for us. To make this clearer, we must pose ourselves a number of new questions:

Do we prize the Eucharist as the bread of life, as the epitome of being for and with one another, as it deserves? Do we do all that is possible to make the celebration of the Eucharist attractive, beautiful, and make it speak to us, so that it can really be experienced as the great family event of the children of God being with one another? Do we feast our spirit richly on the Gospel, on the Word of God? Do we let ourselves be totally taken up by the Eucharistic Christ into his all-encompassing solidarity of salvation? Do we, does the Church in general, do all that is necessary to make the regular living celebration of the Eucharist accessible to all?

We must also sometimes pose ourselves very banal but also unavoidable questions: must not many Christians be ashamed of their physical over-nourishment? Still more serious is the question: have you not stuffed your minds with all kinds of unnecessary or even dirty junk? Is your mind, as the celebration of the Eucharist wishes it, a shrine, in which praises to God continually rise? Or is it not much more a junk-room, full of a grandiose muddle, if not, a robber's den, in which bitterness, grudges and hate have plundered everything. As bread no longer truly tastes good and nourishes, where God and the neighbour are no longer thanked, so a mind that is not flooded with gratitude is no longer capable of taking part in the love-feast of God.

How many parents go to great pains to pile all kinds of presents on their children and leave behind a rich inheritance for them, but do nothing or very little to make them capable of taking part in the precious inheritance of faith and the common meal of love with Christ. They 'have no bread' in the worst sense.

Christians who stand in the Eucharistic core community are utterly prepared to share their surplus with the poorest in the poorest countries. But many have not yet fully comprehended that the Eucharistic community can also require something from them, to insert themselves in political and economic life and help to form of public opinion in favour of sharing the goods of the earth more just amongst all peoples and races, and see to it that all are given the chance to take part in an active, healthier economic life.

A mere sixth of the population of the earth, the Northern people who call themselves 'developed', use four-fifths of the non-renewable, most valuable raw materials and thereby pollute the whole earth with four-fifths of all environmental pollution, including the worrying increase in the hole in the ozone layer. Thus we sin or quietly allow others to sin to an expressible degree against the 'bread', the well-being, and the health of future generations.

Something is wrong if no energy for a deep-rooted change flows from our prayer for bread in the *Our Father* and our Eucharistic celebration with the Lord, who characterised himself as bread for the life of the world. A radical re-thinking and an equally radical change in our expectations of living must come from the all-encompassing perspective of the petition for bread. It is 'our' bread, the bread of all people, and the honour of our common heavenly Father.

The prayer for bread opens up wide horizons for us, which inevitably ask us whether we are really serious in honouring the name of God, the Father of all, in our lives.

It is not a matter of one slice of bread more or less. It is about the worship of God in spirit and in truth, about the familial justice of humanity in the face of God, and without this it is unthinkable that we could have that peace for which Jesus prepared the way through his Gospel, his life and death. All the basic requests in the *Lord's Prayer* are concentrated in every prayer of the *Our Father*.

What will become of our planet?

In the prism of every petition of the *Our Father*, the ecological issues, which in the end come down to the existence or not of humanity, rouse our conscience to full wakefulness and readiness, to an active responsibility for the future of our planet. If that is not the case with us, I fear that our faith and our prayer are salt without savour, light under a bushel. I invite you here to see the whole of the ecological problematic in the prism of the prayer for bread of the *Our Father* together with all the biblical statements about Christ as the bread of life, and the promises that we shall all take part in the heavenly banquet. In so far as you can in this short span of life, put this into practice radically, in a synthesis of prayer, faith and life.

With all the knowledge and capability that humanity has acquired in the course of history, and with the clear vision that faith and Christian prayer give us, could it not be possible for humanity to make the planet entrusted for now to our generation, into a kind of paradise? It could be beautiful and healthy, a magnificent inheritance for the next generation. In reality humanity seems to be hard bent on poisoning the atmosphere, squandering the raw materials, yes, making the whole planet uninhabitable in the course of a few decades.

Naturally, technical and scientific problems and not inconsiderable problems of organisation and politics contribute to this. But the decisive question is whether humanity, believing Christians above all, in their own lives become radically converted to gratitude for the gifts and talents God has entrusted to us, to that solidarity of salvation, that is illuminated by all that the holy scriptures say about the gift of bread.

Prayer

Gracious God, giver of all good gifts, I am distressed that the prayer for bread and the celebration of the bread of life has not influenced my life, our lives consistently. All too often have I simply irreverently repeated the formula. Other times I have perhaps thought more about 'my' bread than our bread. Have I not got stuck at the mere concern for bread, for earthly goods? Yes, every time that I thoroughly reflect on the Our Father, *especially the prayer for bread in the light of the whole Gospel and in the sight of the whole human family, I can no longer rightly understand myself and no longer dare to ask for forgiveness. Help me, help us all, to re-think, turn again, and dare to live a life that corresponds to our prayer and faith, whatever the cost.*

6: Forgive us our trespasses, as we forgive those who trespass against us

*'Lamech said to his wives, Ada and Zilla, hear
me well! Hear what I say to you:
I have struck down a man for my wounds,
a young man in revenge for a small weal.
If Cain is avenged seven times, then Lamech is
avenged seventy-seven times.'*
(Genesis 4:23-24)

*'Then Peter came to Jesus and said, "Lord, if my
brother sins against me, how often should I forgive
him? As much as seven times?"
Jesus answered him, "I say to you, not seven
times, but seventy-seven times." '*
(Matthew 18:21-22)

THE BOOK of Genesis shows us in the example of Lamech how the chain of despising women, ostentation and violence links together. That is how the 'Flood' came to pass: 'but the earth was corrupted before God: the earth was filled with acts of violence' *(Genesis 6:12)*. 'Then God spoke to Noah: "I have decided to make an end of all flesh; for the earth is full of violence" ' *(Genesis 6:13)*. In the course of the last million years, as a consequence of ostentation, vengeance and a lust for domination, humanity again and again has been on the brink of the abyss. Today this advanced generation for the first time is really in the position not just to be able to destroy humanity, but all life on the planet, either through massive ecological sins – slow death – or by nuclear weapons – rapid death. Now it is high time for turning back, which Jesus announced in the horizon of the whole history by his 'forgiving seventy-seven times'. He himself is the absolute embodiment of limitless forgiving.

The words of Jesus on the cross, 'ABBA, Father, forgive them, for they know not what they do' *(Luke 23:24)* are so unheard of that many later copyists of this early text of Luke's Gospel left these words out. To them they seemed simply unbelievable. And yet, they are the gist of the good news of redemption. This is the unsurpassable revelation of the saving, forgiving love of God. Jesus knows that he is not sent by the Father to judge, but to save (cf. *John 3:17*). Jesus is the absolute embodiment of the forgiving love of God.

In the fifth petition of the *Our Father*, Jesus shows us not only the most certain way to obtain the forgiveness of our sins, but also our exalted call to participate actively in the work of reconciliation and peace. To become, so to speak, sacraments of reconciliation.

The drama of redemption

Again and again in the course of history human beings have made their gods in their own image. The
experience and the concept of judgmental justice,
which so often conceals the desire for vengeance by
the mighty, were transferred onto God. This idea
also crept into theories of redemption, which were
(rightly or wrongly) ascribed to St Anselm: according to which the avenging justice of God demanded
that the sin of Adam and the sins of his posterity be
atoned for by the blood of his only-begotten Son.

It is self-evident that everything that Jesus did
and suffered infinitely outweighs any bill which God
might add up from the sins of all people. But God
does not enter into the drama of redemption in
avenging justice, but rather for the justice of the name
of the Father. He owes it to no one but himself, his
fatherly love, that he sent his Son into the sinful
world.

Jesus is above all the unsurpassed revelation of
the saving, healing love of God, the boundless compassion of God for sinful, sick humanity. How much
certain theologians and translators of the Bible were
caught up with, not to say possessed by, the idea of
avenging justice, is shown by an almost unforgivable
but not uncommon mistake in translation in the
fourth Song of the Servant *(Isaiah 53:10)*: 'and it
pleased the Lord to crush him with suffering'. *The*

New English Bible has it correctly: 'the Lord took thought for his tortured servant and healed him'.

In the drama of redemption God shows himself to be in solidarity with the sick, sinful world. With his beloved 'servant' (Son) he shows the world the way to healing and salvation, the way to healing, peacemaking love. 'He was scorned but did not return it, he suffered but did not threaten ... He bore our sins on his body ... Through his wounds you are healed' *(1 Peter 2:23-24)*. The Son of Man/Son of God has come to make friends of sinners, and of enemies who were caught in falsehood and violence, free sons and daughters of God.

The forgiveness of God, as it is visible in Jesus, pays the highest price in buying our freedom from the servitude of conflict, revenge, falsehood. We cannot marvel enough: God loved us sinners so much! He has shown us and prepared for us the way to true freedom, reconciliation, and healing through his beloved non-violent Son, who was willing to suffer for us.

The steep path to peacemaking love

God forgives us sinners, who through our multifarious sins had to a certain degree become his enemies. His forgiveness does not happen in secret. It is a healing and liberating forgiveness. He has made it into the greatest and most meaningful public event of world and salvation-history. His peacemaking love, which makes sons and daughters out of enemies, is the core of the drama of salvation, the drama of redemption, embodied in Jesus Christ: 'he is our peace' *(Ephesians 2:14)*.

In his Son made human, God in human form throws himself into the breach. This is the incomprehensible, ineffable risk of divine love in the face of humanity erring and tangled up by sin. Precisely in this we find the unsurpassable revelation that 'God is love'. In its inmost core and at its highest peak, it is a love that makes friends of enemies. God has loved us, while we were still his enemies *(Romans 5:8)*.

It lies in this mysterious 'logic' of divine love, that reveals itself in the drama of redemption, that God on his side expects and demands from us not only that we love our enemies, and indeed in the creative form of peacemaking love, but even makes this the criterion of whether or not we are really prepared to become his sons and daughters. This is no 'imposition' handed down from above. Certainly it comes from the Father of light, but it comes directly to us through the non-violent, reconciling, healing Servant of God, who became one of us, to take us by the hand and show us the way.

'But I say to you: love your enemies and pray for those who persecute you, so that you might become sons and daughters of your Father in heaven … You should therefore become perfect, as your Father in heaven is perfect' *(Matthew 5:44-48)*.

69

At the time of early Christianity, in Greek culture, God's 'perfection' meant the sublime distance of the unmoved mover of all things. That means not only that God is absolutely impassable, but that he is free from every stirring of compassion and mercy. It is in this cultural context that Luke translates the statement of God's archetypal perfection in the following way: 'therefore be full of compassion as your heavenly Father is full of compassion' *(Luke 6:36)*. It is the empathy of the Father for the lost Son.

It is in precisely this light that the *Our Father's* prayer for forgiveness should be seen. The clause 'as we forgive those who trespass against us' must not give us the idea that God in his forgiveness is measured against our human forgiveness. No, God asks us to forgive through his forgiveness, which precedes it. He always anticipates us in grace. God's own action comes before all prayer, and Jesus' prayer of forgiveness on the cross for the crucified, for all sinners precedes everything. It therefore is incumbent on us to measure ourselves against God's healing forgiveness, God's anticipatory peacemaking love. Yet behind the formulation of the prayer there is an utterly serious warning: if we refuse to forgive one another in God's style, then we are the ones who refuse ourselves divine forgiveness. If we do not want to forgive and yet say this prayer in God's 'ear', that is the most brazen audacity. In short, we say to God: do exactly as I do and refuse me forgiveness! What mad audacity it is to say this prayer in the *Our Father* before God, as long as one bears grudges in one's heart and continues hard-heartedly is animosity.

Do we call down God's punishment on us? In the end it is not God who will punish us. The unforgiving sinner punishes himself, in that he excludes himself through his resentment and discord from God's healing action, and refuses to participate in the work of redemption and peace on earth. A human being must be hard-boiled and unfeeling to dare to proffer a kind of explanation in 'prayer' before God: you, God, forgive me, even if I am not minded to make a serious effort to drive all resentment, all hate and animosity from my heart.

And yet, it remains a terrible riddle that many Christians, who often (or at least sometimes) pray the *Our Father*, do not seriously try to imitate God's healing, forgiving love. I can imagine two explanations: either one prays utterly thoughtlessly and does not seriously pose oneself the question of whether one really wants to forgive following God's example, or the prayer, though honestly said, does not penetrate into the depths of one's heart, or one soon loses oneself again in thoughtlessness.

Let us always reflect on the fact that in comparison to God's forgiveness and the bestowing of peace in the salvation drama of Jesus, the things which we have to forgive one another are really trivialities. Not wanting to forgive or not being able to forgive is a sign of a sick ingratitude to God, but also is a heavy injustice against oneself. Not to want to forgive or not to make an effort to open oneself to the grace of forgiveness is a kind of self-ex-communication. At the very least one excludes oneself for a time from participation in the drama of salvation-history. Worse still: one strengthens the powers of doom and becomes their reinforcements.

A look at the sacrament of reconciliation

It is well-known that for some considerable length of time the sacrament of reconciliation has been in crisis. People find less and less occasion to confess. Many priests also feel uncertain or they put people off confessing with anxious questions about the number and kind of sins.

Without going into the whole complex question, I believe nevertheless I must give a suggestion that might be useful. Through the cultivation of the sacrament of reconciliation and at the same time through honestly praying the *Our Father*, we should gain a clear and fruitful perspective and dynamic, perhaps in the following direction: we all, each and every Christian community, must become a kind of sacrament of reconciliation. We should let ourselves be moulded by the healing, forgiving activity of God. That would be the best penance. Our forgiving, reconciling and healing peacemaking love should become a visible and effective sign that we open ourselves to the saving activity and forgiveness of God. I would like to advise all, but especially anxious people who continually plague themselves with questions about whether they have confessed everything that they should according to the commandments of the Church, to try to redistribute your energies: ask yourself above all, am I on the way to becoming a living, convincing sign and image of the healing, forgiving love of God?

God is unsurpassed in forgiveness. Let us make a serious and persistent effort to become images of the forgiving, peace-making love of God, so that we might be absolutely certain that God can deal with us with even more immeasurable generosity.

If we have grasped this sense of direction, then we will prize the sacrament of reconciliation more and more and it will become above all a celebration of praises of God's healing work.

Struggle against every form of irreconcilability

Every kind of irreconcilability, bitterness and resentment is a dangerous robber, that implants itself in the mind, desecrates it and plunders it. A thankful and reconciled mind on the other hand is a shrine in which the praise of God ceaselessly rises up. It is a source of power, an open canal, through which countless graces flow unremittingly.

The irreconciled and bitter are sick people, and indeed not only in the spiritual or religious sense, which of course is the worst. They are psychologically sick and far more prone to physical illnesses than reconciled, peaceful people. They are dangerous to others in their family, Church and world. They are miserable creatures who destroy themselves and make themselves increasingly incapable of saying 'ABBA, Father' warmly and honestly and happily.

Christians who are irreconciled and embittered through and through must ask themselves what they are daring to say before God, when they say, 'forgive me, as I forgive others.' In short, they are saying: you can not forgive me at all, as long as I remain irreconcilable.

Invitation to the Kingdom of the Beatitudes

God's forgiveness is healing, liberating and peacemaking. The prayer for forgiveness has its tone and its resonance in the realm of the *Beatitudes*: 'blessed are the peacemakers; for they shall be called sons and daughters of God' *(Matthew 5:9)*. Behind the prayer for forgiveness stands Christ, the peacemaker and the praise of all who have let themselves be drawn in ever after into the mission and promise of peace. One does not heal wounds simply by not striking new wounds. God heals through his Shalom, through his peacemaking loving care, establishing healthy relationships. He wakes trust as well by the power of his promise of peace for the peaceful as well as their healing power in all interpersonal relationships. So not only this prayer of the *Our Father*, but all our prayers should be a thankful and committed assent to our mission of peace.

At his baptism Jesus committed himself before God and all the world to his calling as the non-violent Servant of God and of peace; and so too should our prayer keep our grateful assent alive, to serve true peace in all things with Jesus.

It is a dangerous heresy to maintain that the Sermon on the Mount and especially the *Beatitudes* in particular only apply to private life. The baptism of Jesus in the Jordan, in the water, in the Holy Spirit and finally in blood on the cross was no private matter between God and the soul, but rather an eminently historical act. The *Our Father* has a decisively political note. It also demands a continually deepening self-commitment, and letting oneself be committed through God in world- and salvation history.

This petition of the *Our Father* addresses a central dimension of God's plan of salvation. It is a grateful and trusting assent to the will of God, that his peace shall triumph in the world.

If we pray consciously in union with Jesus, the non-violent Servant of God and beloved Son of the Father, in the sight of the Holy Spirit, who renews the face of the earth, in the sight of the Creator of heaven and earth, then we will not be troubled by the temptation to divide the peace of our soul and our family sharply from the public responsibility to peace. The *Shalom*, the peace which Jesus announced, for which he prayed to the Father and for which he gave up his life, is all-encompassing. Correspondingly our prayer as well as our fundamental option for messianic peace must be all-encompassing. In that way the whole Sermon on the Mount, indeed the whole Gospel and especially the *Our Father* marks itself off radically against a privatisation of religion. That would wickedly contradict our zeal for the honour of God, for the glorifying of the name of the Father, for the coming of the Kingdom, which the Father has made over to his Son and to us, his plan of salvation (*Will*).

Christian, awake and rejoice without cease, if you can honestly and truly say, 'Abbuni', our Father, take us into your healing and liberating forgiveness, into your peace. Our irrevocable assent makes us indeed into children of your Kingdom and to joyful messengers of your peace.

Prayer

Unfortunately I must acknowledge before you, Father, that I have often said this prayer very superficially, if not indeed thoughtlessly. Therefore up to now it could not mould my whole life, my thinking and doing and all the features of my life, to my detriment and to the detriment of the world and the Church. Give us all a grateful heart and a grateful mind. Then it will gradually become obvious to us that we depend faithfully on your peacemaking love, your healing non-violence. Then we could break out in jubilation and praise, in the confidence that you recognise and acknowledge us as your true sons and daughters.

7: And lead us not into temptation

The meaning of this petition is shown best perhaps in the words of Jesus: 'watch and pray, that you do not stumble into temptation.'

(Matthew 26:41)

AN EXHORTATION in the Letter to James prevents a certain misunderstanding: 'happy the one who holds firm in temptation. For when he proves himself, he will win the prize of life that is promised to those God loves. None should say, when tempted, "I was tempted by God". For God can neither be tempted to do evil, nor can he tempt anyone to do evil. Each is tempted by his own sinfulness, that lures and traps him' *(James 1:12-14)*.

Temptation that troubles and might beguile us must be sharply distinguished from the testing that enables us to prove ourselves. Earthly life is a place of testing, the arena in which we must show ourselves worthy of the victory prize. Indeed it is true on the one hand that eternal salvation is the unearned grace of God, but in accordance with his wondrous plan of salvation God wants us to mature and prove ourselves in the tests of life. What is pure grace in itself God also wants to give us as fruits of our faithful love.

According to the Letter to the Galatians, in the arena of our testing and proving ourselves, two irreconcilable powers stand opposed: on the one side, the lures and blowing of the grace of the Holy Spirit, the life-giving Breath of the love of the Father and Christ, on the other side however the beguiling forces of the deep-rooted selfishness of the individual and the collective. Collective selfishness and the selfishness of the individual threaten to fuse and band together. Paul names the 'works of deep-rooted self-ishness' to unmask them and warn us. They are above all 'fornication, gross indecency and sexual irresponsibility; idolatry and sorcery; feuds and wrangling, jealousy, bad temper and quarrels; disagreements, factions, envy ...' *(Galatians 5:19-21)*. The apostle warns us urgently against these temptations by referring to the second petition of the *Our Father*, 'thy Kingdom come': 'those who behave like this will not inherit the Kingdom of God.' He does not leave it however as a naked warning. The tone of the apostle's advice emphasises positive encouragement, in looking at the working of the Holy Spirit: 'the fruits of the Spirit are: love, joy, peace, patience, kindness, goodness, trustfulness, gentleness and self-control.' It all leads to this attractive invitation: 'if we have life through the Spirit, then we also want to follow the Spirit' *(Galatians 5:22-25)*.

As soon as we let ourselves be taken hold of and encouraged by the live-giving Breath of the love of the Father and of Jesus, the temptation from the side of deep-rooted selfishness is unmasked in its misery and danger.

The Christian strategy in the struggle against temptation

An ethic predominating in prohibitions, a one-sided warning and talk of evil pre-programmes us for defeat in a sinister way. Such a tactic fixes our gaze on temptation, which on its side continually mobilises the deep-rooted selfishness of the individual and group all over again. Stubborn selfishness, which is continually provoked all over again through loud and one-sided warnings, defends and contracts itself. The loud, harsh orders of an ethic of prohibition have the power to conceal and drown out the healing, saving powers of grace, the lures of the Spirit of God.

The main point of a specifically Christian moral proclamation and pedagogy is the predominant attention on the Breath of the love of God, which lures and encourages us towards the good. The Bible calls this the Paraclete.

Corresponding to the blowing and lures of grace is a quite definite ethic of virtue. It in no way amounts to an individualistic doctrine of virtue, which only concerns itself with self-development and saving oneself. The workings of the Spirit of God are characterised through and through by the solidarity of salvation. All God's gifts of grace and every kind of blowing of the Holy Spirit call and lead the sons and daughters of God to exist for one another and with one another. Of course it is always a matter of my salvation and being saved. This exists and realises itself however only within the solidarity of salvation. Christian virtue is a fruit of the Spirit, which works in all and through all.

Christian virtue as a fruit of the Spirit shows itself in the liberating passion for the coming of the Kingdom of God, in the trusting and decisive assent to God's comprehensive plan of salvation, to which we assent again and again in a deeper way, when we pray: 'thy will be done!'

The commitment to return to thinking in terms of the solidarity of salvation and action is already expressed in the two preceding petitions for our bread, our forgiveness, our peace. If we fall away from saying 'us', in the solidarity of salvation, in order to revolve around 'me', we are already hopelessly stuck in the overpowering temptation that comes from our individual egoism and collective selfishness, and that is spurred on by it.

Virtues which are salvation-historical, seen entirely as a question of solidarity, are the irreplaceable provisions for the struggle against the powers of doom. They protect us from thoughtlessly slipping into temptation which endangers salvation and from every kind of weak and cowardly desertion from the struggle for salvation and against all doom which threatens us.

We cannot remember often and clearly enough the dimension of the solidarity of salvation that is a part of Christian virtue, of fitness in the struggle against the powers of doom and their temptations.

Faith, hope, love

In faith we turn full of trust and dedication to our Father, the Father of our Lord Jesus Christ and all those who are redeemed. We honour the holy name of the Father above all in participating in the realisation of his plan of salvation and the saving concern of Jesus for all people. Faith as an empowerment given by God for salvation-history takes us up into the community of faith and the common worship of God in spirit and truth.

The salvation-historical 'divine' virtue of hope in no way revolves around one's own salvation of the soul, but is rather a grateful, happy assent to the redemption of all people, an abiding in the one hope common to all of us.

In the divine virtue of love we let ourselves be grasped by the love of the one God and Father, the one Redeemer and the one Holy Spirit. It is authentically and specifically Christian only in the participation in the realisation of the love of God for all people.

Gratitude, vigilance, readiness
and the gift of discernment

The four cardinal virtues of Aristotle and the Stoa can be misunderstood all too easily in an individualistic and static way. The salvation-historical virtues of Christian revelation are in sharp contrast to this. They welcome us as those who gratefully receive, those who are grateful fellow-workers, into the one, inseparable history of salvation. Salvation-history and the corresponding attitudes to virtue have three dimensions: past, present and future.

The virtue of gratitude and of grateful praise is the canal through which all the goodness that God has worked in and through humanity flows. This includes gratitude for the activity of God in creation and through creation for us. Gratitude opens our eyes more and more to all the good favours that are intended for us, but also opens our eyes to our responsibility.

In this connection I want to mention the problem of ecology which is so urgent today. It is unthinkable that a grateful human race and in particular grateful Christians would rob and devastate our planet. Ingratitude drove humanity – symbolised by Adam and Eve – out of the Garden of Creation. The lack of gratitude of the solidarity of salvation has devastated and poisoned the earth. The virtue of gratitude, understood in a Christian way in the solidarity of salvation, would thoroughly heal us from ecological blindness and irresponsibility. It would open our eyes to the threatening evil of a worldwide ecological collapse and the increasing devastation of our planet.

How could the Christians of the northern hemisphere, if they were graced with the gratitude of the solidarity of salvation, continue to seize 80% of the unrenewable resources of the earth for themselves and at the same time produce 80% of the pollution of our planet?

The eschatological virtues of salvation-history which refer to the here and now and are recommended to us unceasingly, are vigilance, readiness and the gift of discernment, to interpret the signs of the times and act accordingly. They concern all of us, but especially those who have taken up responsible roles in the Church and society. The 'conciliary process' which we must devote ourselves to much more intensively in ecumenical solidarity and honest dialogue with all religions and groups of people, concerns peace above all, worldwide justice and the protection of the creation entrusted to humanity.

The question of women also belongs to the signs of the times which concern justice and peace. The discrimination against women in society and partly also in the Church is increasingly seen as a sin against justice and peace. If women had had as much say as men, perhaps things would also be in a better state as far as the protection of creation, the ecological virtues are concerned.

Hope and responsibility

The virtues of the solidarity of salvation which refer to the past and to the here and now (gratitude, vigilance, readiness, gift of discernment) only become evident when connected to the virtues related to the future: hope and responsibility. Every attempt at reducing the Christian virtues to a mere ethic of obedience to the detriment of an ethic of responsibility is an assassination attempt on the here and now and still more on the future.

Prayer that is true to life and zealous for the truth must open our eyes above all to the fatal temptations that Jesus clearly unmasked in an unsurpassable way in fasting and prayer immediately after his baptism in Jordan *(Matthew 4:1-11)*. They are the real 'satanic' temptations, that more than anything else want to totally falsify religion and even prayer.

The first of these temptations which is disguised as 'religious' is the distortion of the purpose of religion. 'If you are the Son of God, then command these stones to become bread' *(Matthew 4:3)*. Jesus should prove his Sonship of God by catering to a religion for profiteers. Religion, even in its last fundamental truths, should portray itself as profitable and therefore appealing. Whoever gives themselves over to that and indeed thereby attains positions of honour and power in the Church is a wolf in sheep's clothing. If I honestly pray, 'lead us not into tempta-

86

tion', then my faithful conscience forces me not only to protect myself from this malicious temptation, but also to strive in solidarity with all true worshippers of God to unmask this temptation everywhere where it has nested.

The second of these sinister 'pious' temptations is the distortion of the purpose of religion not only in general, but of the Christian faith in the Son of God, for the gain of power over others in the name of God. This temptation is sinister and cannot be overcome, unless we are all very vigilant about our motives and radically convert to follow the humble suffering Servant of God.

The third truly satanic temptation is pseudo-religion, the ostentation of religious insignia and titles. It is a strange form of self-satisfaction – in the sense of 'self-abuse' – precisely through the distortion of the dimension of the 'holy', piety, ecclesiastical service. The ones who pull the strings of this satanic temptation are skilled in the work of inventing all kinds of insignia and titles, that ultimately are a slap in the face for the humble Son of God.

All those who enter into the service of the Church and its care of souls should study and meditate thoroughly on the whole history of the Church and theology in view of these three of the most common and malicious 'satanic' temptations. I have the suspicion that in the past for many men of the Church their strange concentration on the sin of 'self-abuse' (in the sixth commandment) was a mechanism to blind themselves from seeing the satanic temptation of self-satisfaction through a 'religion of habit' and 'pseudo-religion'.

Prayer

O God! When I seriously reflect on all that, I am frightened. How superficially have I prayed so many times, 'and lead us not into temptation', without reflecting seriously how deep and comprehensive this petition of the Our Father *is! How often have I prayed for the victory over temptation, without bidding farewell to all 'ifs and buts', without giving a full assent to the solidarity of salvation and vigilance. Lord, open all our eyes, that we may not slide into temptation blind and deaf!*

8: 'Deliver us from evil'

EVIL SNOWBALLS dangerously in an entanglement of doom. It cannot be overcome by any who have not committed themselves firmly to the solidarity of salvation.

Many think, when they conclude the *Our Father* with this petition, solely of the evil spirits, the fallen angelic powers. They fear the devil, or the devil without, more than the entanglement of their hearts and activity in all the many powers of doom in a selfish and individualistic world and way of thinking.

Some translations of the Bible refer in the last petition of the *Our Father* to 'the evil ones'. But all official texts of the *Our Father* known to me speak of the victory over evil, over all the powers of doom disguised in this or that way, to which we fall prey, if we do not radically convert to the solidarity of salvation in Christ.

Conquering evil with goodness

The meaning of the last petition of the *Our Father* is perhaps best made accessible by a text from the Letter to the Romans: 'do not requite evil with evil. With all people think about what is good. Insofar as

89

it is possible, be at peace with all people. Do not avenge yourselves, dear brothers and sisters, but leave that to God ... If your enemy is hungry, give him to eat; if he is thirsty, give him to drink. If you do that, you will heap glowing coals on his head. So do not let yourselves be conquered by evil, but rather conquer evil with good' *(Romans 12:17-21)*.

The gathering of glowing coals is an image of the housewife that in the evenings carefully gathers together all the glowing coals so that the fire does not go out. The whole admonition has its full sense and its penetrating power in view of the healing, liberating, peacemaking love of Jesus, the non-violent humble Servant of God. Only in his foot-steps and trusting in his grace can we show ourselves to be peacemakers and thereby sons and daughters of God. As soon as you descend to the same level with evil that reveals itself in hatred, revenge, abuse, and violence, you are lost.

Jesus committed himself solemnly and publicly at his baptism in Jordan to the Father's plan of sal-vation. And the Father confirmed him as his beloved Son at the baptism in Jordan and still more solemnly by his resurrection, after his baptism of blood on the cross. Through our own self-commitment to the healing of love of peacemakers, we enter into the realm of God's plan of salvation, and become thereby Jesus' friends and fellow workers, and show ourselves to be beloved children of God.

The united power of peacemaking love, of healing reconciliation reveals itself in gentleness and non-violence. It is persistent, patient, tolerant. It always reaches out to the opponent in trust, again and again. We see it at its best in Jesus, who even after the traitor's kiss called Judas 'friend', and thereby invited him yet again to be his friend. We see it above all in Jesus on the cross, as he prayed for those who crucified him, for all of us sinners: 'Father, forgive them!'

Even when the non-violent love of peacemakers does not effect a quick and easy victory, it continually works in those who persistently put it into practice as their great protective power in the struggle against evil. If numerous believers consciously unite towards the common goal of this kind of reconciliation and peacemaking love, it bears much fruit for the salvation of the world.

Whoever only thinks of himself and of his own protection against destructive evil from the outside cannot escape so easily from the circle of doom. If however we place ourselves decisively on the side of Christ and, trusting in the saving power of his non-violence, fight against evil in ourselves as well as in our neighbour – also in our opponents – then the circle of doom is broken. We conquer evil through the power of good, hate through the power of love.

In the light of our baptism

If we understand Jesus' baptism in Jordan as his total dedication to his call as the non-violent suffering Servant of God, and finally as the great victor who conquers evil and all its poison through the power of radical love, then that is the first and indispensable step to the full understanding of our own call at baptism. If Jesus at his baptism perceived the call of the Father, 'you are my beloved Son, on you my favour rests' *(Isaiah 42:1)*, and correspondingly committed himself completely to his 'will', to the Father's plan of salvation, to conquer evil through radical goodness, then we also understand our sublime call of baptism that way, for the salvation of the world and thus also for our salvation.

From beginning to end the *Our Father* is at once total prayer and a total self-commitment to God's plan of salvation. It is our life's programme, insofar as our faith and our prayer are true to life. We will not gain quick and easy victories, especially as long as we are still not grasped and penetrated utterly by God's plan of salvation. Certainly it is the case that in the conquest of evil, we might be tempted from the inside. But we may not doubt for a moment that our radical participation in the victory of Jesus over evil through the power of goodness also makes our life fruitful for the salvation of the world.

There is no private redemption, no limiting the healing love of peacemakers and liberating non-violence to our own self and our own little circle. In the end, the whole of the *Our Father* is about the all-encompassing plan of salvation (will) of God, for his Kingdom, for the glorifying of his Father-name. Each and every one of us has an irreplaceable calling to the all-encompassing drama of world-history, which is ultimately concerned with the victory of good over all powers of Doom.

The greater the perils for humanity become as a consequence of injustice, conflict, and damage to the planet which cannot be made good, the more urgent it is that Christians everywhere understand that we can and must enter irrevocably and radically into God's plan of salvation: to unmask evil in all its forms and disguises and to conquer it with united powers through goodness, through a life lived according to the *Beatitudes*.

From the realisation of the *Our Father* in our lives our faith grows in the power of the love of God, in understanding our glorious calling in Christ, in trust and confidence that we can participate in the great victory of good over evil. Thereby we also unmask false self-love.

With every *Our Father* that we pray attentively and with our whole heart, it becomes clearer to us how in our whole life we can honour the name of God the Father, how we can and must struggle for the coming of his Kingdom of love, justice and peace.

93

We commit ourselves anew to his glorious plan of salvation forever, trusting in God's grace. We set out more and more consciously on the way of salvation shown us by the *Beatitudes*. Nourished by the word of God and the Eucharistic bread of heaven, we break open the walls of the prison of egoism and narrow-minded group interests. Gratefully receiving the forgiving and healing love of God in praise, frees us from all resentment, from every kind of lasting grudge and unforgiveness. Full of trust, we pray for power from above, to fight the good fight and to conquer evil in every form through the power of good.

Prayer

God, our Father, we praise you for the superabundant redemption which you have prepared for us in your beloved Son Jesus Christ. Make us grow together with the love of the Redeemer, the peacemaking love of Jesus, to unite and to fight the good fight everywhere where necessary, with the weapons of love, of forgiving and healing non-violence. Free us from all hard-heartedness and keep us from being closed up in ourselves. Let us always understand better how our own salvation is wrapped up in and hidden in the solidarity of salvation, in the common struggle with the 'weapons' of goodness, to unmask and disempower evil. Amen.

9: Praise and programme for life

THE *DIDACHE* (teaching of the twelve apostles) reproduces the text of the *Our Father* similarly to Luke and Matthew, but adds as a conclusion the phrase of praise: 'for thine is the Kingdom, the power and the glory, forever and ever, Amen.' Joachim Jeremias and other well-known exegetes suggest that as a prayer of the community the *Our Father* spontaneously turns into the praise of God. If it does not happen spontaneously, a previously written prayer of praise is ready at one's disposal.

Synthesis of prayer and our life's programme, intercessory prayer and praise

When we emphasise that the *Our Father* is also a magnificent programme for our lives, it certainly has nothing to do with moralism. Moralism creeps in wherever the synthesis between faith, life and our life's programme is absent, and a mere 'thou shalt not' is deemed to be sufficient. Authentic Christian prayer is always and everywhere an integration of faith and life. Therefore it seems particularly important to me to be careful that the *Our Father* reflects this synthesis and thereby takes in petitionary prayer as well as our life's programme in rejoicing before God and in expressions of praise.

Jesus' cry of rejoicing: 'ABBA, Father', resonates in the whole of the *Our Father*. We rejoice, because we may join in this cry of rejoicing, all the more so as we know that the Holy Spirit himself takes us up into the praise of Jesus.

The *Our Father* is good news, the living programme of the Christian community and every single Christian, a confident petition, and from the beginning to the end the praise of God the Father, with the voice of the Son and in the power of the Holy Spirit. That is also appropriately expressed in our joyful singing in the solemn Eucharistic feast of the *Our Father*.

'For thine is the kingdom'

In prayer the Spirit of God himself takes up our weakness. The authenticity and dignity of prayer comes from this, it becomes the worship of God 'in spirit and in truth'. It becomes praise and an expression of life in Christ.

Our prayer as well as our life comes from the basic experience that 'everything is grace'. All power comes from God.

The Kingdom for whose coming we pray is grace, unearned gift. Then again it is also a pressing invitation to work with all our power, trusting in the power of grace for the coming of the Kingdom of grace, of peace, of joy. Above all it means demolishing suppression, saying farewell once and for all to false self-reliance and every form of individual and collective selfishness and boasting.

The honest praise, 'thine is the Kingdom', frees us from every kind of narrow-mindedness as well as all weakness. Jesus takes us by the hand in this petitionary prayer that again and again becomes praise. We should be happy and feel honoured that we are also permitted to work with him trusting in the grace of the coming of the Kingdom of God. The knowledge that all finally depends on God makes us in no way indolent. On the contrary, we let ourselves be taken in mightily in the working of God, and all the more so as we are shot through by the spirit of praise.

'Thine is the power'

If in prayer we look with boundless faith on Jesus, the Servant of God, in whom the Kingdom of God is incarnated, then we begin to marvel how Jesus embodies power in weakness, in gentleness, in the non-violence of one who is willing to suffer. Thus in us the praise 'for thine is the power' becomes a continually new and pressing invitation to follow Jesus for the first time truly on the way of gentleness, of non-violence, to place our trust in God's power alone in sickness and suffering, a power which is revealed so uniquely and unsurpassably in Jesus' willingness to suffer.

In this perspective, praise becomes a firm anchor of hope and of trust. 'I can do everything in the one who strengthens us.' The power that urges us from within and from above to be true to the *Our Father's* programme for life, flows to us in praise for God's mighty grace, which has attained its victory in the humble Redeemer Jesus Christ and powerfully invites us to follow him.

The never-ending praise of the power and might of grace, that revealed itself in the humble, non-violent suffering Servant of God, liberates us also from involvement in every form of selfishness and boasting.

Obviously in praise our humble petition must also resonate with our whole life, thinking, speaking and acting, so that they might be moulded by this very praise of the wonderful ways of the grace and power of God.

Marvelling, thanking, praising opens us to power from above, liberates us from narrow-mindedness and despair. It also moves our emotions and minds towards trust in God and the longing for the coming of the Kingdom of God and the fulfilment of God's wonderful plan of salvation. Marvelling, thanking, praising are irreplaceable basic forms of our petition: 'hallowed be thy name!'

Not long ago I prayed with a ninety-year-old nun who has placed her whole life at the service of the disabled. With a deeply-moved voice she said for a long time 'marvelling, thanking, praising', so that a spark of emotion ignited me as well. Might this living spark remain and ignite in us at all times!

'Thine is the glory'

'The glory of God' is a central notion in the Old as well as the New Testament, and obviously also of Christian liturgy.

The glory of God, *kabod* YAHWEH, animates almost every page of the Old Testament. It is God's overflowing glory of love, that lights up all his days and works. It gives the created world its beauty, its brilliance, its true fullness of meaning. The pious, who are seized by an intuition of a reflection of the glory of God, experience a mysterious harmony of holy terror and boundless jubilation. The reflection of the holiness of God, his glory, has the power to let us experience at once a distressing awareness of sin and the experience of his mercy and grace.

Whoever has begun to experience the glory of God can cry and rejoice at once, be happy and start out on the right path. Such an experience is expressed in our life's programme as: 'all to the greater glory of God.' *(Ad majorem Dei gloriam.)* That is the translation of *kabod* YAHWEH, of 'thine is the glory'. It is a powerful message, to look after the purity of our hearts, our intentions and plans.

This experience, 'thine is the Kingdom', always invites us to examine our consciences again: do I, do we really go about all things praising God's mercy and glory? Can I really bring this or every wish in praise before God?

Examination of conscience

In Christian antiquity up to the time of St Augustine it was not usual for Christians to make an examination of conscience based on the Ten Commandments. With zealous Christians a thorough revision of life is undertaken on the basis of the whole Sermon on the Mount, and goes beyond an examination of conscience to an entire life's programme for the baptised. The daily examination of conscience should take place on the basis of the *Our Father*.

In his Treatise on the *Our Father*, Erasmus of Rotterdam speaks powerfully to the conscience of lukewarm Christians. He calls them 'liars', who dare to lie in God's face with holy words. *Our Father* you say and do not shy away from setting him aside as the Father in all practical respects, only allowing him to be relevant to your own narrow interest groups. Your prayer becomes a screaming contrast to what you say before God. You speak with him about his honour, the honour of his name, but as often as you call on this name, you are bringing shame upon it. Before God you speak of his Kingdom, but even in prayer, alone and in groups, you are more concerned with your own advantage. You do not think once about giving up those things that contradict the Kingdom of peace and justice. You want to give up none of your thick-skulled obstinacy, when you say: 'thy will be done.' You say 'our bread', but mean only bread for you and your fat dog. No morsel falls from your table to the poorest. Even in prayer you do not think once how great your debt of sin is already. You sow discord, in your heart nurse only grudges and hatred and that is all that you give to others as well. You speak without grace when you speak therefore about temptation, and that God should protect you and others from it, while your life and action support a whole system of temptations. And then you still have the shamelessness to ask God to protect you from all evil, while you carry on increasing evil.

At the end of his powerful address on the liars who drum this into God's ears, Erasmus becomes very thoughtful and asks himself nervously whether in the end he himself is also half a liar before God. The same with me. But when we confess and cry to God, 'Lord, save us, for we have sinned' as honestly as Erasmus, then we have the courage to stand stubbornly and trustingly before God, and continue steadfastly and humbly on the way of continual conversion and salvation.

Prayer

Jesus' cry of jubilation and praise rings now in my heart in a new way: 'I praise you, ABBA, Lord of heaven and earth, because you have revealed this to little ones! Yes, Father, thus has it pleased you.' You take the lowly and humble, the non-violent, wonderfully into your plan of salvation and into the praise of your majesty.

Mary, your humble maid, did not sing the Magnificat only once. She herself, and her whole life became a song of praise, completely interwoven with the cry of joy and praise of your divine and human Son.

In the sight of Mary and in boundless trust in Jesus I beseech you, ABBA, Father, take me, take us all, into Jesus' cry of jubilation and into the song of praise of Mary and all the saints. Let our whole life become a song of praise.

It is only trusting in your grace that we may hope that our prayers and praise will transform all our senses and efforts and all our actions. Then we can say to you: and yet I will praise your name. Amen.

'God is humility.'

S<small>R</small> C<small>ELESTE</small> C<small>ROSTAROSA</small>,
F<small>OUNDER</small> <small>OF THE</small> R<small>EDEMPTORISTS</small>